JAMES FORD

Tennis Psychology

How To Build Mental Toughness In Tennis

Contents

1

Introduction

I want to thank you and congratulate you for downloading the book, "Tennis Psychology: How To Build Mental Toughness In Tennis"

This book highlights the importance of mental strength. Mental strength is the mind's ability to focus, to drive the body to perform to its utmost potential. This is the secret weapon to success, to becoming a champion. It discusses the different mental strategies that you can use in order to improve your game and be the champion you so dreamed of becoming.

Everyone has the skill to play. Moves, maneuvers and strokes can all be learned and perfected. However, winning is about the strategy, about the strength of the mind, not just of the body. So how do you harness this potential? This question will be answered in this book.

Thanks again for downloading this book. I hope you enjoy it!

2

What Does It Mean to Be Mentally Strong in Sports?

The world of sports is a tremendously demanding arena. The game can be very tough, not only in terms of the physical demands, but also on the mind. People play not only with the physique, not only in terms of skills, but also in terms of the mind, of strategies.

Athletes do not win merely because of their physical abilities. Victories are not always achieved by being the fastest or the strongest. Athletes become winners because of how they strategized- how they train and play the game using their mental abilities. This is about having mental strength.

Capacity to stay in control and manage temper

In a game, there are numerous possibilities that can make an athlete lose his temper. The audience may be harsh, booing every mistake or any move. A bad serve, a missed shot, getting whacked by the other player, a contested call – all these can cause anyone to lose temper easily.

It can be very easy to get angry and lose your temper on the court. Yelling or smashing your racket right after every miss you make can be very easy to do, but you must not let yourself react before you can compose yourself.

Losing temper does not help in winning the game, or the inability to control emotions. It can only lead to getting more sidetracked from the real focus- in winning. Tempers can get the best of anyone, even top athletes.

In the game of tennis, the hours of exposure to the scorching sun can add to tempers boiling just under the surface, which can easily be triggered to erupt with the slightest provocation. Mental strength includes gaining control of your temper; you should be able to control it despite all the factors that are triggering you to lose your head.

Tempers are emotions that need to be controlled because they can hamper concentration. It can distract the tennis player from playing at the top of his game. It can ruin strategies and cause a player the much-coveted win.

The capability to keep cool despite the intensity of the match very well helps in winning. Despite the hostilities from an audience that clearly loves the opponent, from bad serves, or from just about any unfavorable circumstances help in winning. This ability helps in keeping the focus on the match, on how to strategize to score and win the match.

One trick that is guaranteed to help you control your temper is this: before reacting to a bad shot or any other shot you make, take a few deep breaths. There's a good chance that, after you have composed yourself, you will realize that throwing your racket or losing your temper won't do you any good. In fact, losing control of your feelings could affect the way you play on the court negatively. Learning to keep your cool will help you easily move on from your bad misses and help you focus on what is really important, which is the next point.

Capacity to stay alert

It is easy to lose focus in a tennis match. The heat, the perspiration, aches and pains- all these can easily distract the tennis player. Or, it may be from overconfidence. Previous matches may be too easy. The opponent is underestimated. Two successful and easy sets can make a player overconfident of winning and botch up the third.

A mentally strong player should be able to keep his focus, to be alert at all times. It does not matter if the game is an easy one, with a victory easily up for grabs, or if the game is a tight one. Be alert until the very end. A third match can turn the tide into the opponent's favor.

Capacity to rise above lack of self-confidence

Being a pro at tennis cannot be achieved without having enough confidence in every game you play. Confidence in playing tennis cannot be achieved overnight. It is a journey that you have to go through as you play your sport. Focusing too much on the technical side of the game is not the biggest factor that could help improve your self-confidence. It is your perspective and attitude during every match that affects your tennis confidence.

Let go of the what-ifs. One of the reasons why you become too nervous during a match is because you start jumping into the future instead of focusing on the present. If you let your mind get ahead of yourself, you become more uptight and begin to undermine your self-confidence.

Playing against tennis superstars like Rafael Nadal and Roger Federer can easily bring on a case of self- doubt, of getting intimidated. Having the Williams sisters or Maria Sharapova as an opponent can make you feel star-struck and inadequate.

Remember, if you have trained well, any opponent, even tennis celebrities, can be beaten. All it takes is a winning attitude, the confidence to have what it takes to win. Rising above lack of self-confidence can do wonders to a tennis player.

Why not see things this way: just the fact that you are playing against top caliber players is enough proof that your skills are already that good - enough to be pitted against the top athletes.

Capacity to maintain a winning momentum

Two sets may be too easy, scoring well with little effort. But the tide may turn on the third set, when mistakes after mistakes, series of bad serves can lose the game altogether.

There are games wherein the likely winner loses in the end because the player was unable to sustain his momentum. He lost focus or became too confident of a win that is not yet his.

It is easy to be laid back and become too sure of oneself due to previous good sets. But a winner stays on his toes up until the winner is declared. The momentum is kept going up until series ended. Top tennis athletes keep the competitive edge – they do not slow down just because of an apparent lead.

3

What is Tennis Psychology?

Tennis psychology offers several techniques that help players improve their game. Using different mental techniques when playing can be a great strategy for tennis players of different skill levels. Some of these mental techniques include:

Controlling one's thinking

To increase your chances of winning a tennis match, think positive. Your mindset greatly affects how you play your game. Practicing the mental game in tennis means that one must be in control of his thoughts and not let the negativity take over. Once a player lets negativity kick in, his body would involuntary react the same way.

This is because his ability to reason is being compromised, making him act in ways that are not good for his game. Experts in tennis psychology suggest that a player must stay positive by constantly being aware of his thoughts even when he is playing. The more aware a player is, the more he can develop a positive train of thought.

Some of the things a player can do to keep his positive thoughts in check are: doing positive self-talk before a game point; allowing himself to feel pumped up after getting a point; or simply keeping an enthusiastic attitude during the entire game. One can achieve success by having the right mindset and belief in his own talent. Having faith in your abilities is a vital factor for success and victory.

Limiting your belief in yourself only shows your lack of faith, and could sabotage your chances of winning a match. Never let external factors affect how you react and play your game. Always fight those negative thoughts and push through your strengths.

Having a clear judgment and keeping yourself motivated no matter how your game turns out is very important. It will take a while to master this technique, but once you get the hang of concentrating on the actual game while controlling the mind, it can really make a great difference on the way you play.

Managing one's emotions

Another mental toughness technique is learning how to manage your emotions during a match. Being either under excited or over excited could affect how you play the game. To be mentally fit in tennis, a player must keep a balance in his level of excitement throughout the game. Being under excited would result to being under motivated as well, while being too excited would lead to hasty decisions. A just right level of enthusiasm would help you play to the best of your abilities.

Intangible aspects of the game

Another important mental technique in tennis is identifying factors in the game that are out of your control. These are factors that you want to focus less on. Once on the court, there are several things that could affect how you play that you know you cannot control.

Some of these include the opponent's abilities, the weather, the court conditions, and the audience. You may not be able to control all of these different factors, but you can control how much attention you give to them and how you let them affect the way you play. If you let these factors get to you, you will likely be less motivated and lose control of the techniques that you trained so hard for. You also begin to lose energy that was supposed to be channeled towards your hits and strategies instead of on other irrelevant factors.

Clearing one's mind and refining focus

Focus is an essential part of tennis psychology. A player must be able to clearly focus on his tasks and goals in order to win his matches. In a game, a player can be faced with a lot of distractions, such as the cheering of the audience or even the gestures of the opponent. Do not fuss over any of these intangibles. A huge part of being mentally fit for tennis is refining one's focus to what is important – the game.

The human brain is a great multi-tasker. It can let you work on so many things at one time. When playing tennis, however, it is best to keep all of your brain's focus on the game. Practicing the mental game of tennis would require keeping your concentration on the court all throughout the match.

Most tennis players, especially the new ones, tend to be very focused during the first part of their games. But as the games progress, players begin to lose focus due to many uncontrollable factors like pressures from their environment. Tennis psychology helps players stay focused even during the most difficult parts of the game.

With focus, a player will be able to anticipate his opponent's next move more accurately. Visualizing the opponent's response to your hits will help you apply the best techniques and strategies. With constant practice, a tennis player will be able to master his focus and have a good idea of the most common reactions to their different shots.

Improving one's mental toughness

A tennis player can never win a match if he does not believe in his abilities. When executing shots, physical strength is not the only thing that's important. Your confidence when making a hit also counts. Maintaining confidence is a huge contributor to a strong tennis match.

Mentally tough tennis players are those that are able to execute their strategies well even when they are under pressure. Making yourself appear like you are very confident of yourself even when you feel very nervous also helps. Remaining confident and calm could make you look stronger and could intimidate your opponent.

Being mentally weak could cloud your judgment and make you doubt your every move, even before you execute them, resulting in a loss of time and even your energy. Once you begin to doubt yourself, you give room for your opponent to make more successful hits. Being sure of your actions and techniques is one important mental factor to make you perform better.

Being in the zone

Tennis psychology is an excellent tool to help you get "in the zone" — a place where your mind and your body are at sync. Once you have conditioned both your mind and body, you will be able to gain better focus and execute better strategies for your game. Most players who are able to put themselves in the zone usually end up winning their matches.

A perfect example of a player practicing this mental tennis strategy is Roger Federer. He keeps himself in the zone in many of his tennis matches, a mental technique that helped him win against many other excellent professional tennis players.He does not allow his mind to wander off. Once he is in court, he is able to execute every technique precisely. One example is his proper demonstration of a unit turn — one of the key parts of a tennis technique. A player does a unit turn when both his body and racket moves together as a unit as preparation for a backhand or forehand stroke.

You can get yourself in the zone before a match by following three steps. First, you must silence your mind. Get rid of any worries and negative thoughts that could affect the way you play. Second, you must trust your own strengths. You must apply everything that you learned from your trainings and be confident of your skills. Lastly, stop judging yourself. Winning a match is a great achievement, but losing is also a learning experience that could help you grow in your tennis career.

When used the right way, tennis psychology could help you get an upper hand on your opponent. All these techniques provide you with the basics of being mentally fit for tennis. Applying them could guarantee an improvement in your game and can take you to newer heights. Constant practice is key. Eventually, you will be able to use all the techniques you trained for in the actual game naturally.

It is important to note that every individual's brain works differently. This means that these tennis psychology techniques could have different effects depending on the player's abilities. Each player has different emotions and level of confidence, so it is important for you to focus on the areas of your mind that you know you need to work on. Once you have understood your own strengths and weaknesses, you will be able to use tennis psychology to your advantage.

4

Building Confidence

Building confidence in tennis can be a bit difficult and even some professionals doubt themselves once in a while. To develop this mental toughness skill, start with the simplest ways. Some of these methods can seem common but very difficult to apply, while some could challenge the way you look at things.

The road to achieving confidence could require you to change your attitude, but it can help you reach success not only in playing tennis but also in life. What is important is your willingness to learn and to have an open mind in order to make building confidence much easier. In this chapter, you will discover the steps to building tennis confidence.

It all starts with the mind

Mental training plays a huge role for every game of tennis. To gain tennis confidence, it is important to be aware of the things that go on in your own mind. The first part of your mental tennis training is learning acceptance.

No matter how hard you train, there are times when things might not go your way. It is normal to make mistakes during a match. However, there are times when you make more errors as a result of poor self-confidence. You must learn to accept your mistakes. These are things that already happened and cannot be taken back. All you can do is let them go and find ways to improve your technique.

Accepting one's mistakes can be a difficult thing to do for a lot of people. Sometimes, you don't notice it yourself, and it takes someone else to point out your mistakes. When someone talks to you about errors in your stance, your shots, or your grip, how do you deal with it?

Managing your mistakes

When you make mistakes, do you do something to prevent it from happening again? Do you find ways to make yourself improve? If not, then it means that you were not able to acknowledge your mistakes and learn from them at all.

To manage your mistakes, you must understand how every error affects how you play. You can do this through three steps. First, you must accept the fact that you made a mistake. Second, you must analyze how you can correct it or execute it in the proper way. Third, you must let go of that mistake to avoid repeating that same error.

It is important to be aware of the errors you make and how to make them right because it can help you become more confident. Mistake management allows you to have control over your game. Once you have that sense of control, you will believe in your capabilities more.

Setting your goals

To build tennis confidence, you must set realistic goals. Allow these goals to be challenging, but make sure that these are something that you can achieve with your current abilities. Never set goals that you know from the very start are impossible to reach. It will only make you feel frustrated and discouraged.

To achieve confidence, you must set specific goals that must be achieved at a certain amount of time. By doing this, you will be able to measure the speed and amount of your improvement. Create a timetable of all your goals and record every improvement you make. Once you have made progress, you can start pulling up your game standards. This way, you can level up in every game.

When you go on a cycle of goal setting and achieving your goals, you become more confident because it affirms how you have improved in your skills and abilities. From time to time, take a look at your goal record and you'll realize how much you have grown. This should encourage and motivate you to play better.

Refining your skills

Tennis confidence cannot be achieved without constant practice. The more familiar and comfortable you are with the game, the more confident you will become. Daily practice to improve your skills is important.

Your practice does not have to always be in an actual tennis match. You can practice using a ball machine or a wall, or you can practice with another player through a casual game. When practicing with another player, you must agree on how your game will be played, the drills that you will focus on, and the time you will spend for every drill.

It is only with practice that you will be able to master how the game naturally flows – from your swings to your hits. Mastery of the basics is very important, because this allows you to move with confidence in every game. This also helps you become more in control of your technique, increase the chances of you winning a match.

Focus for confidence

Developing tennis confidence requires developing your focus as well. Practicing your visual and physical contact with the ball can help you concentrate better and improve your focus whether you are moving or stationary. There are many exercises that you can do to help your eyes get used to focusing on one thing even when you are in motion. Try practicing using a ball machine that throws different colored tennis balls and aim to hit only a specific color. You can also practice with a wall while playing a distracting music.

In the actual game, make sure that your focus is on the tennis ball and not on your opponent or the audience. By doing regular focus exercise, you will be able to increase your confidence when playing because you know where the ball is going.

Calming your mind

Developing your mental stability is an important part of building confidence. You must learn how to calm your mind and channel your emotions in the appropriate way before, during, and after your match. Never let your negative emotions dictate the way you should play your game.

To improve this mental skill, you must practice keeping your calm during all your trainings. Getting a bit (or too) emotional during an actual match or even in practice cannot be avoided. There are times when you can get easily frustrated, exasperated, or overwhelmed with what you are doing. These emotions are usually manifested in your failed swings or missed shots. You must not let these emotions overpower you, but it is important for you to be aware of them.

Knowing how to deal with these emotions is vital. Once you become aware of how you feel and what is going on in your mind, you will be able to control them so they don't affect your game. Your tennis confidence develops once you learn how to stabilize your emotions. You will feel unwavering confidence no matter what errors you make during a game. It's really all about perception — how you look at the outcome of your moves can affect the way you play during the next few rounds.

There are a few exercises and routines you can do before a match or during breaks in order to lessen your negative emotions. All you have to do is take deep breaths to help reduce your frustrations. Never let yourself channel your feelings through your hits and swings. This will not make you stronger. Instead, this will only lead to you losing your game in the end.

Consistency is key

As much as possible, be consistent with the way you play. This applies to your techniques, your emotions, and your focus. Once you are able to keep both the physical and mental aspects of your game in check, you will have greater chances that your confidence level will stay high. However, there might be some instances when you could be placed in complicated situations that would require you to re-examine your techniques. This is normal and completely alright to do.

Consistency does not necessarily mean staying in the same position, releasing the same amount of power, or executing the exact same shots all the time. Being consistent means not panicking when your opponent executes something new during a match.

The capacity to stay calm and to be able to work out a stance to respond to your opponent's hit is consistency. Once you have mastered this skill, you will become more confident since you know you are ready for anything that will come your way.

5

Mental Mistakes

At the height of an intense match, tennis players who previously performed exceptionally could suddenly make a series of mistakes, losing a title that they could have easily won. Most of the time, bad serves and missed shots are more due to mental mistakes than inadequate skills. Here are some of the common mental mistakes tennis players make that can ultimately lose a match.

Downtrodden attitude

Do you often try to predict or imagine yourself doing a poor serve or hitting the ball the wrong way even before you actually make a move? Sometimes, when it comes to conditioning your body to play a certain strategy, these mental images can be more powerful than actual words. If your mental images are negative and all you think about is making bad shots, this will involuntarily program your body to act negatively.

You must be in total control over the things you feel and see in your head before making a move. The quote "what you think, you become," is very applicable when playing tennis – if all you think about is missing the next point, your body gets programmed to fail.

A player who focuses on what could go wrong or the mistakes that have been committed is less likely to win. Concentrating on not making a bad serve or is preoccupied with what not to do cannot properly strategize on how to actually win. Matches are won by making a good play, and not on avoiding mistakes. Scoring is not through avoiding bad moves but by how to make the opponent miss a serve or a shot.

Letting emotions affect the way you play

Most people commonly see angry tennis players throwing their racquet when they make mistakes on the court. However, there are also other players who appear very calm and composed although they are already about to explode on the inside.

Frustration is a huge enemy of many tennis players. Once you get frustrated, you start dwelling on all the mistakes you made during your previous sets. Being stuck in your past will prevent you from focusing on your current game. Never allow yourself to get carried away by your negative emotions. It will only cause you to play aggressively, miss a point, or give up entirely.

Overconfidence on strengths

Concentrating too much on strengths can lead to loses. A strong backhand is great, but that is not all that wins a match. Overconfidence in one skill can block the enhancement of others. A player loses the potential to improve a play because he relies too much on a single one. Doing so can also expose one's weaknesses to the opponent. Consistently using the backhand can signal to the opponent of a poor forehand, and he will likely take advantage of that. A winner develops a variety of moves, and do not just concentrate on the strengths. Training should actually put more focus on improving the weaknesses and should not be about mastering an already good move.

Obsession for victories

While it is not wrong to want to win all the time, an obsession can actually hinder success. A mindset that winning is everything can ultimately be a player's downfall. One can easily lose focus when mistakes are made. Frustrations over loses can devastate a player, causing to lose concentration. A person with too much focus on winning can easily get frustrated and disappointed, and be unable to improve his play.

If you lose, take it as an opportunity to think back on what caused the defeat. Losing can actually be beneficial for a champion-in-the-making. Defeats highlight what needs to be improved in an athlete. It reveals the weaknesses that you probably do not even know about, as well as the areas that you still need to improve on.

Over analyzing the simplest things and trying too hard

After making an error, many tennis players try to fix their mistakes. They do this by changing the way they normally play – their strokes, their hits, and their stance. They think too much to the point where they feel like they do not know how to play anymore. This problem among many players is often referred to as 'paralysis by over analysis.' This means that when players think too much, it prevents them from making the right moves.

You should avoid trying to correct your strokes while you are in the middle of your game. That's not the time to think of a new technique to use. This is almost a sure way to trigger panic. Consequently, you end up making even more errors.

This is not to say that you should not switch techniques right in the middle of the game. If you must tweak your strategy to respond more effectively against your opponent's shots, do so using techniques that you have already tried in training. This comes with proper planning and knowing your opponent's style. But, if you have to sort through all the techniques in your arsenal while you are already playing, forget it. That's the worst thing that you can do. You will most likely end up with a worse game.

Remember that the human mind functions best when it processes only one thought at a time. Do all your thinking and planning while you are preparing for your game. Once you step into the tennis court, your mind should only focus on your game. Do not compromise your game by having wayward thoughts clogging your brain and stopping you from doing what you need to do.

Do not analyze your game as you are playing it. You can do that later as you evaluate your game and think of ways to improve. While you are on the game, you must find the simplest ways to get points even if you are not executing your shots perfectly and when you are not playing at your best.

Playing in accordance with the current state of mind

While a winning attitude and a positive state of mind helps in winning a match, playing which is entirely dependent on a current state of mind can make you lose the game. Top players are people who do not just depend on what they are currently feeling. They are able to separate personal and professional feelings and concentrate on the game.

It is not always that an athlete feels good about himself or of the game. There are times that the mood is just not at all positive due to several factors, like personal issues; it could just be that you are simply not up for a game that day. Great athletes are able to maintain their top performance despite feeling unhappy, or being amidst doubts and personal struggles.

Nonspecific goals

Most athletes set out to improve their game, but they do not set more specific goals. Goal setting should be SMART- Specific, Measurable, Attainable, Realistic and Time-bound.

Specify what areas to improve on, like making no more than 2 bad serves in a game. It should be measurable, like getting nine out of ten serves. It should also be attainable. Setting a goal like "I will make no mistake in this game" is not a good idea because it is not attainable.

Nobody is perfect. Embrace the fact that mistakes can happen but rising above it is what counts most. Goals should also be realistic, meaning it is within the realms of reality. It is good to aim to be the best, the most extraordinary, but aiming to be the "best in the universe" is simply not something to focus on. Time-bound means that goals should have a specific time frame.

This helps in keeping an athlete on his toes at all times. This also prevents getting too lax. For example, having a goal of winning this year's Wimbledon is better at focusing all efforts for the current season, rather than a goal of just winning a title, with no specific period or even a title in mind.

6

Mistake Management and Blocking Out Distractions

Players often get too conscious about the way they plan and are nervous about making errors on the court. An effective way to avoid this is to give them a constant reminder that their previous mistakes should be left in the past and should not be dwelt on too much. It is getting that next point that matters. Once this kind of mindset is incorporated into their regular training, it will be easier for tennis players to get into the proper frame of mind during the actual game.

The capacity to be in the moment is a very important factor in winning a match. By keeping the mind in the present, tennis players will be able to bring out the best in themselves and channel their energies effectively into their game.

However, it is not just enough to stay in the present. Players must also give all their attention into the things that matter, that is, their technique and the tennis ball. There can be a lot of distractions during a tennis match. A mentally tough tennis player knows how to block out all these distractions and ignore the things that cannot be controlled.

Attracting confidence through visualization

Visualization is a skill that plays a very important role in the mental game of tennis. Several sports psychologists use visualization to help train athletes to develop their mental tennis abilities. Through visualization, players are made to create and imagine events that they want to happen in their game.

To simply put it, you can picture yourself acing that serve, perfecting a swing, getting better at your technique, and winning your game. Visualization can help improve your self-confidence by making you trust yourself more. It also encourages you to achieve that goal you pictured yourself achieving.

Every tennis player should start practicing visualization no matter what level they are in. You can start by doing some visualization exercises before the start of a match. Spend a few minutes before the game to visualize how you want your game to go.

Picture yourself playing in court and making an excellent first serve. Then, imagine yourself using powerful strokes and swings that make it difficult for your opponent to hit the ball. Lastly, visualize yourself performing the best you've ever played in your entire history of playing tennis and winning your match.

You must keep in mind that visualization does not work simply through imagining things. To visualize, you must make all your senses aware of what you want to achieve. Visualize how your racket feels in your grip and how you would toss the ball during your service. Listen to how the audience would cheer for you after every successful hit, and even be aware of the 'boos' from your opponent's own supporters.

Lastly, imagine how you would feel when you win – the warm feeling the crowd would give you and your exhilaration over your victory. By training to visualize every day, you will eventually develop self-confidence and attract positivity to your game.

Blocking out distractions to be mentally tough

When you are mentally tough, you are able to ignore all the things that could cause you to lose your focus and lead to your defeat. A lot of things could go on at the stands, the adjacent court, and anywhere near the tennis facility, but these are not of your concern and must not divert your attention from what really matters – your current game.

Other natural elements could also affect the way you play. The heat of the sun, the wind, the sunlight blocking your view of the ball, and other factors could be distracting. However, these are things that cannot be controlled and must be taken as things that are simply there. Complaining about them would be useless.

Many other players experience the same things, but, somehow, you feel like it's unfair when any of these happens to you. What you must do is find a way to continue playing despite these natural distractions, because there really isn't much you or other people can do about it.

The entire history of tennis shows how successful players were all known for their mental toughness and ability to put their attention on things that are important. These successful players also know how to channel their energy on things they can control.

If you start to practice this, you already have an edge against your opponent. For a number of players, rituals are important in mastering a consistent mental rhythm with the game and blocking out distractions.

Blocking out distractions also requires self-awareness. If a player experiences fatigue or has any injuries, he must know how to make the necessary adjustments to maintain his focus and to continue playing the game as best he could. Both physical and mental awareness are necessary although they both have to be balanced. It's not just purely 'mind over matter.' When you neglect to address one, you are likely to experience distractions on another.

For instance, as you prepare for your game, you could do your visualization rituals and give yourself an internal pep talk. You're all mentally revved up that you do not feel any hint of jitters at all. The euphoric feeling 'distracts' you from noticing that your ankle is actually a bit sore and might be injured. This bit of glitch in your self-awareness will definitely hurt your game.

Remember that there are things that you can control. It would difficult not to feel regret when you fail because you were not able to pay attention to these things. To ensure that you are not prematurely declaring your readiness without actually going through all the preparations, you need a lot of discipline. By now, you should already have realized that tennis is more than just a physical game. It requires a lot of mental preparation and strategies as well.

7

How to Improve Mental Strategies

A match is won in the mind. Whether in terms of having a winning attitude or strategizing well during a game, mental strength is a major propelling force of winners. How do you improve the game using mental strategies? Take these tips:

Mental Imagery and Visualization

- ### Mental imagery

Focus on what the goal is. For example, "I want to have a strong forehand like a certain top tennis player".

Put your mind on how the top player does the move. Every movement, every stroke is brought to the mind's attention. Every detail should be played over in your mind. Relax the mind and the body while creating this external imagery.

Imagine the self doing that move alongside the player. Picture the self performing the same move. Every detail of the movement should be played over in the mind. Create this internal image and slowly start to prepare the body to be receptive to the sensations stimulated by the image.

Imagine how the body would feel like while doing the shot. Feel the sensations of every movement, each stroke, the swinging of the arms, the pressure on the shoulders and arms, as the racket is swung overhead.

While the movement is played over in the mind, imagine how it would feel as the arms are moved. Think of how it would feel swinging the arms and hitting the ball. Imagine the self in the moment of an actual match - the heat of the sun, the sweat trickling down the back and face, the shout of the audience.

Let the imagery transport the mind, as well the body's sensation into the moment. Go to lengths to visualizing the tennis court, the grass, the net and all other details of the environment.

Internalize the imagery and let the thought translate into sensations. Let the muscles tense up, as if actually doing the backhand and forehand. Imagine holding the racket and feel its weight. Imagine the hands gripping the tennis racket. Feel the tension in the muscles as if swinging the racket to hit the ball. Imagine and try to feel the vibration as the ball is hit and the sound it makes. Think about all the events during an actual match, the pressure, the tension, the adrenaline.

Internalization is recommended until such time that the mind and body are confident and poised to actually perform the act. This usually takes about five minutes. It is also recommended to use mental imagery early in the morning, when the mind is relaxed and the body is refreshed from a good night's rest. Doing this will allow the positivity to follow through the rest of the day, and be adequately used during trainings, as well as during a match.

· **Visualization**

This is seeing within the mind how you want something done, how you exactly plan to carry out a particular action. It is very much similar to the mental imagery. The only difference is that you consciously plan every act of the mental image, instead of using experiences as a basis for the mental experience. In mental imagery, you recall the events and the sensations that accompanied them. in visualization, it is more of looking towards the future, of how you would want something to happen.

Some sports psychologists believe that this method is more effective. The athlete gets to have a clear picture of a tennis match, and gets to plan out the moves, the strategies without having to fatigue the muscles.

In using mental imagery and visualization, the muscles are primed for action and the body is pumped with low doses of adrenaline, to keep it toned. Doing the imagined acts in reality can lead to build up of lactic acid in the body, which leads to fatigue and lowered performance. By using imagery, the athlete gets to have a low dose of body conditioning, with the same muscular tension and the adrenaline action, but not to an extent as to stimulate the production of lactic acid. This chemical is produced by the body when the muscles contract for a longer period. It tends to build up and cause fatigue, and even cramps and other muscle injuries.

Relaxation exercises before and during a match

Many players tend to feel very nervous and anxious before a match. In addition, other players could get very emotional after getting a point and others when they make errors. Some would even reach the point where they would throw tennis balls to the crowd, bang their rackets on their heads or break them with their hands. When players do this, they are unaware that they are spending so much of their energy in releasing their emotions and they eventually lose focus.

This is where relaxation techniques come in. These can help you avoid having negative emotions prior and during your game:

· Listening to music

Relaxing the mind is essential to develop mental toughness in tennis, especially before the start of every match. If your mind is bothered with a lot of things unrelated to your game, there is a huge tendency that you will lose concentration. When you relax your mind, you will be able to have more focus for your upcoming match.

A lot of players would listen to certain types of music while they are on their way to their competitions. Some would listen to relaxing instrumental music, while others would listen to songs with motivational lyrics that they can relate to.

· Breathing exercises

Mental training for tennis also requires knowing how to control your own body. Doing some breathing exercises is one way to help you relax your anxious mind and body. This technique for mental toughness is very important and needs to be done prior to and during the match.

Taking deep breaths is a practice that players should turn into a habit. Many experts recommend inhaling and then exhaling slowly. In each breath, they have to practice awareness in order to calm your body. Professional players would usually take their time before making a serve so that they can relax both their mind and body. Breathing exercises could also help you control your temper in the court.

· 10-minute silence before a match

This tennis mental exercise simply requires you to find a place where you can spend a few minutes of quiet time. Allow yourself to have at least 10 minutes of silence to contemplate before you go to your game. Simply sit down, close your eyes, and relax. Clear your mind of negativity and let yourself be more aware of your body. After five minutes of sitting in silence, start doing some breathing exercises until you feel ready to play your game.

Self-hypnosis for improved athletic abilities

Hypnosis is defined as a state of mind where three things exist - the mind's intense concentration on a thought or idea, the relaxation of the body, and the increased vulnerability to suggestion. It is considered as a state of exaggerated suggestibility. Hypnosis can be used in athletes like tennis players. During the hypnotic state, suggestions are given which are treated as ideal solutions that will help you become the best athlete you could be.

Self-hypnosis is achieving a hypnotic state on your own, and the hypnotic suggestions come from you. The only downside is that you may be giving yourself thoughtless or negative suggestions. Train your mind to think only positive, helpful thoughts. Otherwise, self-hypnosis may be less beneficial than intended.

Self-hypnosis is different from meditation. The latter is clearing the mind from all distraction. The mind, as well as the body, becomes more relaxed, focused and balanced. In self-hypnosis, the same effect is achieved. In addition, the tennis player can give himself suggestions that can easily be carried out by the mind and the body.

De-cluttering of the mind makes it, as well as the body, more receptive and able to follow through the hypnotic suggestions. The ideas are better received as compared to merely telling the self of these suggestions in a preoccupied and troubled state of mind.

Self-hypnosis is another aspect of the mental tennis game. Nowadays, several major tennis academies have designated certain parts of their training all for mental tennis training. Self-hypnosis on court is a tool used by many tennis coaches to train players with higher level of experience.

When playing tennis, how you feel during the game is a huge determining factor of your performance. What this means is that during every match, your emotions and thoughts must be in sync in order for you to perform at your best. There are many professional players seen using self-hypnosis during a match.

The things that you tell yourself during your game can greatly affect your performance. This is effective because most of the time, the things that you say are expressions of the things that you think about and the emotions that are embedded deep in your mind. If you are able to manifest the positive emotions within you through your words, it will hugely help you in your game.

One way through which you can develop a positive self-talk is by doing it even during your practices. To improve your chances of winning your matches, you must tell yourself positive things. Use some words of encouragement like telling yourself that you are capable and that you have the right skills to win your game. Tell yourself to avoid getting angry or frustrated, and to prevent complaining when some little things don't go your way. Lastly, tell yourself to stay focused no matter what happens around you.

Self-talk is very helpful especially when you start to feel down during a match. It can really help bring back your motivation especially during tournaments when you have to be all on your own.

The mental aspect of your game can be positively reinforced by self-hypnosis. This practice does not make one do things beyond what he is capable of doing. It is merely a way to unlock the hidden potential, to go beyond perceived limitations and reach the utmost possibility. Self-hypnosis does not provide superhuman abilities; rather it releases the unrealized abilities that have been kept hidden and unused.

How to perform self-hypnosis

To start, look for some place that is quiet and relaxing, where you are least likely to be disturbed. Lie down or sit, as long as you are in your most comfortable position. Make sure you will not be disturbed, so turn off phones and alarms, shut and lock the door and put up a "Do not disturb" sign.

The time you allot to self-hypnosis is up to you. Most recommend around 15 to 30 minutes. Know your goals and think about them as you prepare for self-hypnosis. Fix you gaze at a certain point, on a blank wall perhaps. Keep staring at this fixed point while you relax your entire body.

- Concentrate on the awareness of your eyelids. Slowly and repeatedly tell yourself that your eyelids are getting heavier. Let them close when you feel you can no longer keep them open with minimal effort.

- Be aware of the tension in the body. Start with the toes. Think of the tension slowly draining from the body towards the toes.

- Relax the toes, the feet and work it upwards. Relax the body in parts, until every part is calmed and soothed.

- Take deep breaths. With each exhale, imagine the tension being released as a dark cloud. Each inhale brings in a bright energy that slowly fills your being.

- By now, be aware of your relaxed body.

- Picture yourself standing on top of a flight of stairs with 10 steps. Each step takes you to the tennis court. By the fifth step you can see the court.

- Picture the tennis court. Imagine yourself picking up your tennis racket. Feel the weight as you tighten your grip on the handle. Flex your arm holding the racket and take a few practice swings in your mind.

- With your mind's eye, look around. See the stands and notice the audience. Hear their cheers.

- Look at your opponent (or the top player you admire the most). Imagine him standing on the opposite side of the net, taking a few practice strokes himself.

- Take the remaining five steps to enter the court. Imagine yourself picking up a green tennis ball. Feel its roughness and roundness. Bounce it a few times on the ground. Feel the rhythm, the sound it makes as it bounces off.

- Imagine hearing the sound of the whistle, the signal to start the game. Imagine yourself doing the first serve.

- Bounce the ball a few times on the ground and hit it with the racket. Feel the vibration of the ball as it hits the racket. Send it flying over the net to your opponent's side.

- Play the match in our mind. Visualize each hit, each stroke. Feel the sensations as the muscles tense up and make each stroke to send the ball flying off. Imagine each detailed movement, exactly how you want each stroke to be executed. At this point, tell yourself your goals. "I want the serve to sail smoothly past the net." "I want the forehand to powerfully return the ball."

- Take note that as you play the match in your mind, concentrate on what you do in the scenario. Do not attempt control your opponent's reaction. Let that part of the scene go because like in reality, you cannot control what your opponent does. Let this also be true in your self-hypnosis. Concentrate on your moves, and not on how your opponent reacts. Avoid thinking "I will make this serve and he will trip over his feet." This is not going to work. Remember that self-hypnosis is to help you reach your optimum level and not be a venue for wishful thinking.

- Gradually feel your heart racing, the same adrenaline rush when you actually play a tennis match.

- Then, as the set comes to a close, slowly tell yourself to gradually relax, to cool down, as you would in an actual game. Take deeper, slower breaths until your entire body relaxes again.

- Slowly take the 10 steps back to where you started. Once back, tell yourself to slowly open your eyes and return to reality.

8

Maintaining Top Performance While Under Pressure

Tennis matches and other sporting events get very competitive. The pressure mounts, especially during championship or title games. Athletes sometimes lose not because they lack the skill or did not train enough, but because the pressure was too much for them to bear. They crumble under the expectation and the demands of the game on their minds, not on their bodies.

Champions win not just because they have superb abilities, but because also they have trained their minds to keep on the top of their game. Some top athletes have average physique and abilities. What brought them to the top spot of their sports is their mental abilities, the mental strength that they posses. This strength enabled them to bear the pressure and keep performing at their best. To harness your own mental strength, follow these simple tips:

The power of positive thinking

Negative thoughts find their way to the front and center of consciousness at any time, most often when you least want them to be. The pressure of winning can weigh down on the mind. Self-doubts can creep in right before a match or even during the game. All these negativities can block your path to success. Any thought that crosses your mind has an immediate effect on the cells of the body. A negative mind will translate to a negative body- a poorly functioning one that cannot maximize its abilities. Trainings and techniques will be forgotten or executed poorly if the mind is unable to give the needed push.

Control your mind. Do not allow the negative thoughts to have free reign on your mind. Be aware of your train of thoughts. Direct these to positive patterns. Before going out on the court, talk positive things to yourself and fill your mind with positive thoughts. Think of your goal and how you plan to do it. Remind yourself of the strengths you have and embrace your weaknesses. Find your inspiration and keep your focus on it. Do self-talk before and even during the game. Keep the effects of distractions to a minimum. Recognize that distractions will always be there and you won't be able to a lot about it. What you can control is how you react to it. Concentrate on what you should do, and not worry about the results. Regardless of the score, keep your drive to perform better, to make better serves. Avoid thoughts like "don't do a double fault" because that is what exactly will happen- have a double fault.

Emotion control

Too much excitement or less enthusiasm can significantly affect your game. Too much giddiness will cause you to lose focus and make impulsive decisions. You also tend to spend too much energy on the feeling, which deprives the body of the energy it needs the most. Less enthusiasm can make your serves lousy. Maintain just the right amount of emotional energy. Strive to maintain balance.

Do deep breathing exercises. Overcome the stress and tension. Concentrate on the moment, on each point made. Do not dwell on the mistakes. Let go of the finished moves, there is nothing you can about it. What you can do is make the next move count into your advantage.

Learn what you can and cannot control

There are things you simply cannot control. For example, you cannot control your opponent's moves, his serves, the way he hits the ball back to you, or even the weather. Let go of these things. Dwelling on these can make you lose focus. You will be wasting your energies that can otherwise be used to strengthen your game.

Concentrate your efforts on the things you can control. Be aware of your serves, strokes and scoring pattern. Learn to adjust your moves as the situation changes. And keep yourself positive, your energy well spent on the things you can change and control.

Be in the moment

Anxiety can mount as the game progresses, especially if your opponent's scores are steadily rising over yours. Do not be distracted by this. Think that the other player is also having anxieties and pressures of his own. The game is won not by the scorecards but by how each player deals with their own anxieties. The better player is the one who keeps performing well even with the mounting anxieties and pressure of the game. Keep your cool. Dwell in the present moment.

Play by sets and stop worrying about the previous or the future set. Stay in the moment and concentrate on how to make each of your moves count. Dwell on each stroke, in how to hit the ball and not on how your opponent reacts to your moves. Stay focused on your own side of the court- not on what is happening on your opponent's side, nor on the stands.

It is a reality that not all people watching in stands are on your side. Some are inevitably rooting for your opponent. A few boos should not distract you. Train your mind to stay on your side of the court.

9

Dealing with Cheaters

Seeing your opponent cheat can be very upsetting. But, cheating is something that you could encounter at some point in your life, whether in competitions or in other areas of your life. When your opponent starts to cheat, he is not only being dishonest and breaking the rules, but he is also taking away a point that could have been yours.

When this happens, some athletes get pissed off and become emotional. As a result, they are thrown off their game and the cheaters often 'steal' the entire game from them.

Tennis players and other athletes cheat for many reasons. They could do it because they feel too much pressure about winning and fear dealing with defeat. Some do it simply because they are used to it and do not feel any guilt at all when they cheat. Others claim that they are not aware that what they are doing is considered as cheating.

Whatever the reason is, what matters most is how you are able to handle situations when your opponent is a cheater. This chapter will discuss two ways to deal with cheaters.

Remain calm and don't let them affect you

A person's natural reaction when faced with someone who is cheating is to get enraged and lose control over his emotions. Once you let this happen to you, you will sabotage your entire game. Allowing cheaters to get to you – making you emotional and out of control of your actions – makes you lose your focus on your goals.

If you let yourself be overpowered by your emotions, this will eventually affect your performance and you will be unable to execute your techniques effectively. Instead, you must learn to keep your calm both mentally and physically. Keeping yourself relaxed even when you are under pressure is essential to achieve peak performance, so you must channel your energy to staying cool.

To do this, you can start by relaxing and taking control of your breathing. Show your opponent that his act of cheating did not affect you. Even if you are enraged inside, make it look like you are calm and composed. If you want to call your opponent out, you can do so but in a calm manner. Make sure too that it is in a manner that is acceptable based on game rules. Remember that your opponent could actually be intentionally cheating to irritate you and throw you off your game.

Maintain control over what you must focus on

Cheaters are experts in distracting their opponents. They have their ways of knocking off your concentration from the game so that you would fail on your next shots. Through cheating, they cloud your mind with negative thoughts like anger and frustration, effectively spacing you out from the actual game.

Never allow them to take over your thoughts. You must try your best to resist getting distracted and keep your focus on what you must do – which is to win the game. Instead of letting cheaters get to you, direct your attention to getting the next point.

Lastly, always keep in mind that people who cheat do so because they are incapable of executing strong techniques on their own. Cheaters usually do what they do because they feel insecure and are threatened that they might lose. They know that they cannot win the game by playing using their own strengths, so they find other dishonest ways to get points. When you encounter a cheater, think of it as a chance for you to stay calm and show them what you can do.

10

Conclusion

I hope this book was able to help you to be aware of the secret weapon to win in tennis, or in any sport for that matter. Mental strength is not just a myth or a belief, it is a reality that can ultimately help you reach your full potential and use it, even in the heat of a match.

The next step is to start practicing and strengthening your mental abilities. Remember the old adage, What the mind can conceive, the body can achieve.

Finally, if you enjoyed this book, please take the time to share your thoughts on Amazon. It'd be greatly appreciated!

Thank you and good luck!

CONCLUSION

The trademarks that are used are without any consent, and the publication of the trademark is without permission or backing by the trademark owner. All trademarks and brands within this book are for clarifying purposes only and are the owned by the owners themselves, not affiliated with this document.

Printed in Great Britain
by Amazon